Images of
Wolverhampton

Express & Star

Images of Wolverhampton

Breedon Books
Publishing Company
Derby

First published in Great Britain by
The Breedon Books Publishing Company Limited
44 Friar Gate, Derby, DE1 1DA.
1995

ISBN 1 85983 038 2

Printed and bound by Butler & Tanner, Frome, Somerset.
Jacket printed by Premier Print, Nottingham.
Colour separations by Colour Services, Leicester.

Contents

Introduction

WOLVERHAMPTON has no grand cathedral, few ancient ruins and, for all its size, is not even a city. Yet it has been around for more than a thousand years and it takes pride of place in the industrial heritage of our nation. It was once known as the 'Workshop of the World' – and rightly so.

Here, for centuries, were the furnaces and forges that fuelled a dream. Here, in unlovely terraces and smoke-blackened factories, was the raw energy which helped to build the United Kingdom and the British Empire.

And yet even in those dark and often satanic days, sanity and tranquillity were only a stroll away. The town may have its roots in the bustle and grime of the Black Country but it borders the glorious unspoiled countryside of Shropshire and Staffordshire. Nowhere in England do the interests of town and country come into contact – and sometimes into conflict – quite as they do here. In every town-bred Wulfrunian is a countryman with the race-memory not merely of steam hammers and pig-iron but also of lurchers, ferrets and poacher's moons.

In the year 985 King Aethelred granted lands here to Lady Wulfruna. In 994 the town's history officially began when she made a gift of land for the establishment of a monastery. By 1078, following the Norman conquest, the settlement earlier known as Heantun (High Town) had become Wlurenehampton. Over the next two centuries it grew in importance and influence receiving, in 1258, a Royal Charter for the holding of a weekly wool market.

Wool brought great wealth to the growing Wolverhampton, perfectly situated as a large market town so close to the sheep-rearing lands of Shropshire and Wales. But as Yorkshire began to dominate the woollen industry, the future for Wolverhampton lay increasingly with coal and iron and the dawning, in nearby Coalbrookdale, of the Industrial Revolution.

Everything changed. The town beloved of drovers and herdsmen, the town whose wool wealth is commemorated today in the street names which end in 'fold', was thrust into a new and more brutal prosperity. Wolverhampton began the eighteenth century with a population of 7,454 clustered around the market place. By the end of the century the number of residents had doubled and their little settlement had become a fully fledged industrial town, turning out consumer goods for the Empire and hardware for the mines whose pit-heads suddenly sprouted by the dozen in this coal-rich region. John Wilkinson developed a revolutionary new blast furnace at Bilston in 1756. Twenty-two years later the town's corporate life began with an Act of Parliament appointing Commissioners for 'the good order and government of the town'.

They did the job well. During the nineteenth century clean streets, proper sewers and pure mains water steadily wiped out the cholera epidemics of the early Industrial Revolution. Commerce and culture flourished in Wolverhampton. Parks were laid out, fine schools established and stately crescents sprang up for the newly-rich and their families. It was a time of great ideas, passionate religious beliefs and a groundswell of radical, anti-Establishment politics. If ever a man found his time, and his town, it was Scottish-born Thomas Graham who moved south with his family in the 1840s and who, in partnership with the legendary Scottish-American millionaire Andrew Carnegie, founded the *Express & Star* in the 1870s.

Carnegie believed that the industrial regions of Britain, including the Black Country, were ripe for his brand of Republicanism. As he observed on one depressing ride through the region: "The eleven miles between Birmingham and Wolverhampton are nothing but one vast iron-working, coal-mining establishment. There is scarcely a blade of any grass of any kind to be seen. Oh, mills and furnaces and coal pits and all the rest of you, you may be necessary but you are no bonnie."

Carnegie's Republicanism did not take root but the newspaper he founded went on to become Britain's biggest regional evening newspaper, reflecting the changing face of a unique town and region.

Part of that change was the emergence of a world-famous football team. Wolverhampton Wanderers, a founder member of the Football League in 1888, has run up a string of Cup, League and European victories and given the game such legends as Stan Cullis, Dennis Westcott, Bill Hartill, John Richards, modern-day hero Steve Bull and, of course, the late, great Billy Wright.

Wolverhampton provided endless munitions for both world wars yet was hardly bombed. Its nemesis came in the 1960s and 1970s when its ancient heart was torn out and replaced with concrete, all in the name of progress. By the 1990s it had reached an uneasy alliance with the motor car which had almost destroyed it and the Wolverhampton of today (rose-tinted nostalgia notwithstanding) is probably a more comfortable place to live, work and shop than at any time in its 1,000-year history. A remarkable town of remarkable people. This is their story.

Peter Rhodes,
September 1995.

Grateful acknowledgement is made to Diane Hurford of the *Express & Star* Editorial Support Department for her work in collating the photographs for this book.

The Streets of Wolverhampton

Dudley Street on 12 July 1949 in a sweltering temperature of 85 degrees.

A tram at the Tettenhall terminus about 1908.

The Hen and Chickens, Snow Hill, Wolverhampton, in September 1933. The building has now been demolished.

A view of the building which housed the probation office staff, taken from the Newhampton Road East, Wolverhampton, in February 1967.

In April 1946 the Mount, Penn Road, was acquired as central headquarters for the youth services of Wolverhampton.

Royal London Mutual Insurance Society Ltd building, in Princess Square, January 1967.

The Barnhurst
Farm House,
December
1960.

The derelict Lodge Farm, Goldthorn Park, Wolverhampton, October 1967.

The Ministry of Labour Employment Exchange, November 1966.

September 1966 saw the opening of The General Accident Fire & Life Assurance Corporation Ltd's new branch offices in Waterloo Road, Wolverhampton.

Central Library,
January 1970.

Civic Hall, January 1968.

Popular with shoppers in July 1967 was Wolverhampton's Central Arcade.

May 1953 saw the shopkeepers and business people of Wolverhampton give the town a colourful aspect for Coronation Day. In this Wolverhampton arcade shopkeepers banded together to buy decorations.

Wightwick Manor, April 1958.

The Coach and Horses around 1910. It stood on the corner of Bell Street. The site is now part of the Wulfrun Centre.

A picture of the Quarter House in Compton Road, Wolverhampton, painted by a local artist, George Phoenix in 1883.

The Rose and Crown, Penn, 1906.

The Molineux Grounds, 1871.

The Star and Garter Hotel, Wolverhampton, February 1935.

The old dole house in Bee Lane, Bushbury, June 1950.

Castlecroft Lodge, November 1967.

Martins Bank, Waterloo
Street, July 1968.

A group of men gather to discuss strike action at a local firm outside the Percy Thomas Hall in July 1962.

The Drill Hall at West Park in October 1967.

This photograph, taken in May 1959, is of 62 Bath Road which is thought to have once been the old toll house to Wolverhampton Racecourse.

Cleveland Court Club, March 1966.

Wolverhampton's Victoria Street in 1910.

A reminder of the past on the new Bushbury estate was this black and white farmhouse at Northcote, Wolverhampton, pictured in December 1953.

Queen Square, the heart of Wolverhampton, was under reconstruction causing bottleneck traffic during December 1950.

Castle Street, Wolverhampton, 1964.

A miniature park being carefully nurtured in the middle of the traffic island at Chapel Ash in September 1952.

Bell Street,
September 1961.

This 'rooftop vista' taken from the Royal London Mutual Society's building in November 1951 looks down Stafford Street and shows Bushbury Hill on the horizon.

Chapel Ash roundabout in May 1957.

The sharp corner between Bilston Street and narrow Garrick Street which was unable to cope with traffic in May 1964.

A familiar scene to generations of Wulfrunians in October 1954 were these shops in North Street near the centre of the town.

Residents of Monmore Green, Wolverhampton, set off on horse-drawn waggons for a well-earned outing in 1913 .

St John's Square, September 1949.

Queen Square – the Changing Face

Mr T.H.Roberts, Wolverhampton Art Gallery Curator, in June 1954, examines the painting of Queen Square in the early nineteenth century. The picture was bequeathed to the town.

Queen Square in 1820.

Queen
Square
around
1824.

Queen Street, 1890, looking towards Lichfield Street.

Queen Square in 1894

Looking towards Lichfield Street with the Art Gallery of 1884. This picture of Queen Square was taken in 1902.

The hurly-burly of traffic could clearly be seen in this picture of Queen Square in 1921.

An everyday shopping scene is captured on this picture of Queen Square on 8 October 1931.

A busy day for Wulfrunians is captured in Queen Square in 1944.

Queen Square in June 1964
before the zebra crossing was
removed.

About 25,000 plants were put into this beautiful emblem which was a floral tribute to the golden jubilee of the Toc H movement in August 1965. At the centre is the lamp of maintenance which figured in Toc H meetings.

A general view of Queen Square in 1965.

Queen Square approaching Lichfield Street in April 1969.

Going to Market

Workmen giving Wolverhampton Market Hall a spring clean in April 1953 found the town's original coat of arms. The discovery was made when they climbed above the doors of the building to take down boardings which for many years covered the archways.

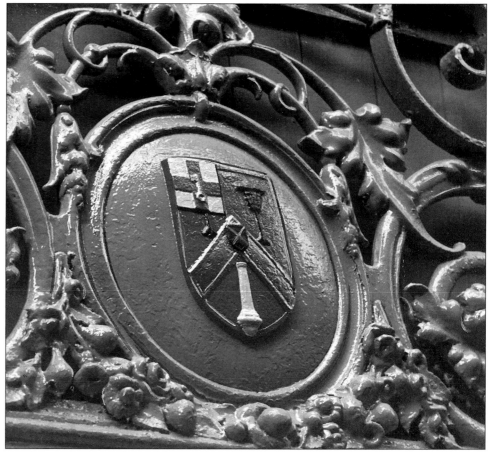

Women in 1850 referred to it as the 'Market Patch'. In the twelfth century the patch was in Queen Square. In February 1957 it sprawled in the shadow of the grey-stoned St Peter's Church.

Looking down on demolition work at the old Market Hall from the top of St Peter's Church in January 1961. In the background, left, can be seen the Town Hall. The top of the Civic Hall is in the centre.

The Market Patch with the Market Hall on the right pictured in August 1953. The picture was taken through the archway of the Education Offices. These gates are no longer in existence.

The Market Hall site in July 1954.

Wolverhampton's 'new' open market was one of the liveliest places in town every Saturday in 1962.

The Wholesale Market in Wulfruna Street in June 1963.

Taken in 1965 this picture shows
the fountain on the old Market Hall.

Lord Morrison of Lambeth on a visit to the market in Brick Kiln Croft in June 1960. The market cost Wolverhampton Town Council £500,000.

An end of an era for the Wolverhampton Market Patch in May 1960. This picture shows shoppers on the last but one market day.

Easter shopping at Wolverhampton open-air market in March 1956.

An aerial view of Wolverhampton open-air market in November 1956.

In May 1960 the last market cries were recorded. Here Mrs Edith Taylor is pictured recording her voice.

Mr Norman Pritchard speaking at a public meeting in the Market Place in June 1944.

Wolverhampton Market Hall
pictured in April 1958.

Wolverhampton Market Hall in December 1952.

A view of the
deserted retail
market in
Wolverhampton
taken during a
Friday
afternoon in
August 1967.

The tea garden at Wolverhampton's retail market in February 1962.

Crammed shoulder to shoulder with each other shoppers waited to be served in Wolverhampton's market in December 1961.

Stall holders preparing for another day of trading at Wolverhampton market in 1953.

People, Places, Events

Moseley Old Hall pictured in 1947 after being taken over by the National Trust. Charles II hid in the house after the Battle of Worcester.

Swans and ducks on the ice at West Park, Wolverhampton, in January 1946.

In February 1954 children enjoyed sliding, skating and sleigh rides in the snow at West Park.

Northwood Park Cottage which formed the lodge entrance to a modernised Northwood Park in August 1955.

An Empire Day gathering outside St Peter's Church in the 1920s.

The foundation stone laying of Low Hill Methodist Church in 1928.

An 'airphibian' on Wolverhampton roads in July 1948. It arrived at Wolverhampton Airport and within three minutes the wings had been removed from the metal fuselage front, a canvas hood slipped over the back, and the front part rolled away as a motor car.

The Chinese ambassador and his entourage with the Mayor of Wolverhampton in Darlington Street in 1900.

The first ever degree ceremony held at the College of Technology in June 1967. Here some of the graduates wait for the ceremony to begin.

West Park in 1881. It was built on the site on the site of a racecourse – part of Broad Meadow. It was the venue for the great Art and Industrial Exhibition in 1902 which closed after a few months, making a loss of £30,000.

The Mander family launched a £10,000 appeal in 1937 for St Peter's Church. This picture shows people gathered to celebrate reaching the target.

The broken Elizabethan slab which was on top of what had been regarded as a tomb at Wrottesley Chapel. But in March 1950 the Revd R.A.Lord, curate at the burned-out Tettenhall church, thought it could be an old altar covering the bones of St Thomas à Becket, martyred Archbishop of Canterbury. Mr G.Budd, foreman of Messrs Henry H.Wilcock, builders, is seen inspecting the slab.

The civic procession entering St Peter's Church for the special centenary service in June 1948. The Mayor's Sergeant and a police sergeant are followed by the Mayor, Alderman H.E.Lane, and the Town Clerk, Mr J.Brock Allon.

A few of of the 1,500 children at the Sunday School centenary service at St Peter's in 1948.

In August 1969 this was the end of St Paul's Church which had stood for years as a monolithic landmark by Penn Road. It was demolished to make way for shops, offices and homes.

It was known as the Copper Kettle in the early part of the century but in March 1956 it became the Lindy Lou, a pram shop, situated on the corner of St John's Street.

The Grand Theatre around 1900.

The great outdoors provided the setting for the hustle and bustle of
Wolverhampton's old open square market in St Peter's Square in 1910.

The advertising curtain at the Grand Theatre in the early 1900s.

The drop curtain at the Grand Theatre. The curtain was painted by John Leonard, a scenic artist, in 1915 and took him almost a month to complete.

The new number board at Dunstall Park Racecourse in 1932.

All eyes were on the dogs as they passed the winning post at Monmore Green in December 1969.

Winter sport on Tettenhall frozen paddling pool in February 1954.

Families relaxing at Tettenhall swimming pool in September 1959.

Britain's fastest runner in May 1960, Peter Radford, receives advice from coach Bill Marlow at Aldersley Stadium. Watching (left to right) are John Salisbury, a crack-quarter miler, Ted Aves, Oxford hurdler, and Mike Parker, a Worfield farmer's son who was tipped to reach great heights in the hurdling world.

Wolverhampton's first Territorial WRAC, Miss Barbara Selwyn, being enrolled in February 1954.

Wrottesley Hall's head gardener, Mr Bill Weekes, tends the lawns in front of the house in June 1963.

Wightwick Manor taken in December 1968. The picture shows the elaborate gables, their timbers carved with patterns of Gothic design.

A panoramic view of the Penn golf course and 'common' land in September 1955.

A large audience attended the Civic Hall in December 1961 to hear Handel's *Messiah* by Wolverhampton Civic Choir and a section of the City of Birmingham Symphony Orchestra with Mr Arnold Richardson the conductor.

New Year's Eve Dance at the Civic Hall in 1960.

The opening of the Civic Hall in May 1938.

Down at the Pub

The Crown and Cushion, Bilston Street.

The Talbot Hotel, Princess Street.

The Gifford Arms, Victoria Street.

The Spirit Vaults, St John's Square.

Right: The Old Barrell at
the corner of Bell Street
and Victoria Street.

Swan and Peacock Hotel, Snow Hill.

A group of regulars outside the Wood Hayes, Wednesfield.

The Swan Public House, Compton.

Town at Work

The offices and warehouses built in 1969 for the national company J. H.Sankeys & Son at Strawberry Lane, Wednesfield.

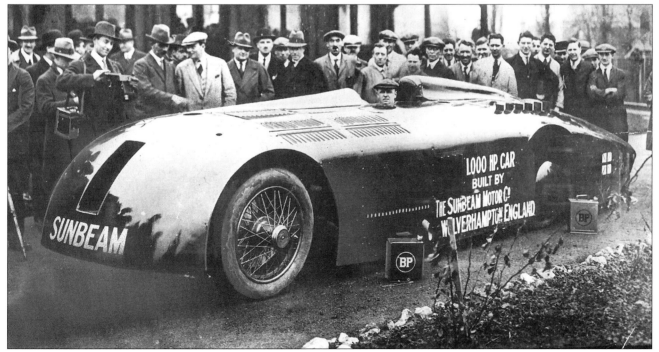

The Sunbeam car that brought fame to Wolverhampton when it crashed the 200mph barrier in Spring 1927 at Daytona Beach, Florida. It was nicknamed 'The Slug' because of its ugly shape.

Yale & Towne building in Willenhall in July 1960. It was the division for the manufacturing of locks
and hardware.

Goodyear's pictured in July 1957. The field in front has now been built on.

A skilled operator at Goodyear's in 1962 checks the continuous length of shaped tread compound for correct width, gauge and weight, before cutting to the appropriate length takes place.

A hemisphere being hot pressed in May 1969 at the Wolverhampton works of the Thompson Horseley Division of the John Thompson Group.

Clergy visiting John Thompson's in Wolverhampton, October 1970.

In September 1964, at Boulton Paul, this was one of the latest airframe jobs to be undertaken for a Beagle 206 executive aircraft.

The smelting furnace at Stewarts & Lloyds Ltd, Bilston, in September 1959.

May 1961 saw the latest addition to the transport fleet of Mander Brothers Ltd, Wolverhampton – these three Guy Otters, two with van bodies and one an open platform truck fitted with Gardner 4LK diesel engines. The makers claimed that the fuel consumption for these vehicles was 27mpg.

James Gibbons founded his locksmithing business in Wolverhampton in 1670. In October 1969 this old hand-operated anodising plant was being made ready for the scrapyard.

Miss Bess Deans, one of the senior staff members of William Gibbons printers, Wolverhampton, is seen hand-printing the cheque serial numbers which had to be placed clearly and exactly on a given point, September 1969.

Mrs J.Harper (right) helped by Jessie Howells gives the final polish to shoes made at Edges Shoe Factory, Wolverhampton in July 1969.

In September 1968 distributors
for Guy Motors gathered at their
Wolverhampton factory for a
preview of the firm's exhibits at
the forthcoming commercial
motor show.

The massive works chimney on
the Bilston steel works is prepared
for felling in 1911. Cloth-capped
spectators watch as demolition
experts prepare the chimney.

Barrels… barrels… and more barrels. Stretching away into the distance this is the scene in Butler's yard in December 1961 as the barrelled beer awaits delivery to the pubs.

A post-1928 Sunbeam Motor Cycle made at its plant in Wolverhampton.

In 1961 these bottles revolved around the filing machine at the rate of 600 dozen every hour at Banks's Brewery.

In 1969 Courtaulds' factory in Wolverhampton, although not beautiful, was screened from residential areas by Lombardy poplars in order to create attractive pictures.

Not a wedding cake but the Aubin Trophy representing a history of lockmaking up to 1851 returned to Wolverhampton in July 1965 to be displayed at Chubb's offices in Wednesfield Road. It was built by Wolverhampton locksmith Charles Aubin who had premises in Poutney Street for the first of the Great Exhibitions in 1851.

A door for a bank's strongroom being made in June 1954 at Chubb & Sons Lock and Safe Co. based in Wednesfield Road.

A segment of the double tube
which Marston Excelsior Ltd,
Wolverhampton, made in July
1961 for nuclear research
equipment at Harwell.

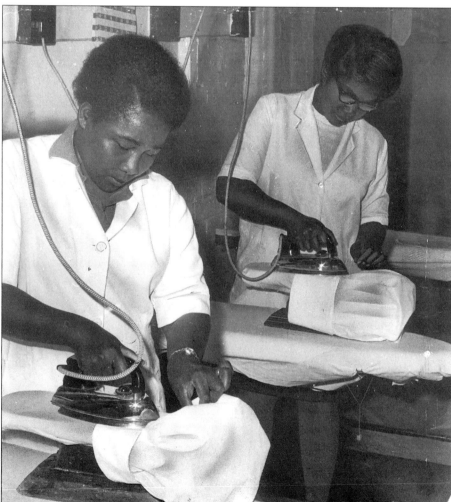

Mrs Maria Murray of Heath
Town and a colleague at work
in Wolverhampton Steam
Laundry in July 1970.

The stalls where washing was boiled and scrubbed in July 1960 at Wolverhampton Steam Laundry.

A typical rotary drier package burner made by Stordy Combustion Engineering Ltd at Wombourne in April 1969. This burner used 250 gallons of oil per hour and was capable of producing more than 100 tons of asphalt per hour.

Casting operations at William Barnsley Ltd in December 1966. The company, founded by Mr William Barnsley in 1890, made the first motor cycle with an engine in the frame.

The exterior of the new office block of Wolverhampton Metal Co. Ltd which fronted on to Rookery Street in May 1962.

In December 1966 this was a general view of the Wolverhampton and Birchley Rolling Mills' new 500-ton capacity bar shearing machine said to be the only one of its type in the UK.

A horizontal borer was installed at a cost of £28,000 at Wolverhampton Auto Machinists in August 1969. It could machine items up to the size of 6ft cubed.

Welding Equipment Services Co. Ltd., Wolverhampton modern and spacious premises based at Lower Horseley fields in June 1964.

A rotary transfer machine made at Wolverhampton Motor Components was capable of performing 18 simultaneous operations on engine accessories including drilling, spot-facing, milling and tapping. Here it is being used at Villiers Ltd in January 1964.

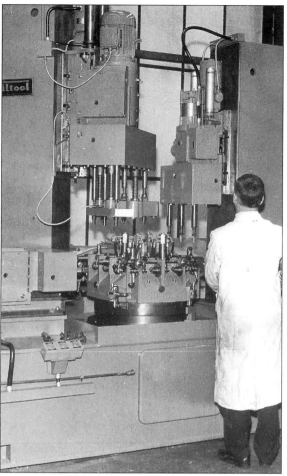

A Midland firm closely connected with the fortunes of the motor industry was Wolverhampton Die Casting Ltd. in March 1957. This picture shows one of seven new conveyor production lines installed to cope with the motor industry's expanding needs.

Civic Collection

Far left: Badge of past mayors, pictured in May 1937, and *left*: Wolverhampton's mayoresses' badge pictured in April 1952.

The Mayoress examines Wolverhampton Corporation silver in September 1949. The 26 pieces were estimated to be worth over £5,000.

The Mayor's Sergeant, Bob Whalley, polishes the mace for the last time in September 1948 after leaving the Town Hall to take up another post.

The mayoral chair pictured in May 1962.

The new badge for the mayor's consort in May 1957.

Pictured in 1957, the silver cheroot was presented to a lieutenant of the Dragoon Guards in 1835 by the inhabitants of Wolverhampton.

Wolverhampton's coat of arms.

In February 1959 the Mayor of Wolverhampton, Councillor J.C.Homer was pictured admiring the silver table centrepiece which was presented to the town by the late Alderman R.E.Probert on his retirement from the office of Mayor in 1938.

An 11-piece silver dessert service pictured in 1958. The service was presented to the late Sir Alfred Hickman by Wolverhampton Conservatives in 1880 and was given as a gift to Wolverhampton Town Council by Mr Edward Hickman.

Working for the Community

Nursing staff pictured outside the Wolverhampton and Midland Counties Infirmary in its jubilee year in 1931.

Royal Wolverhampton School, 1970.

Wolverhampton Grammar School around 1970.

Wolverhampton Municipal
Grammar School, 1967.

The Wolverhampton Territorial Unit – 444 Light AD Regiment – pictured in November 1966.

Panda cars being handed over to two Wolverhampton police divisions in January 1968.

Part of the fire-fighting display at Wolverhampton's new fire station official opening, September 1968.

Loading up the van ready to start delivering the meals in June 1965 are Wolverhampton Meals on Wheels ladies Mrs M.Boon (left) and Mrs N.Wrightson.

Radio operator Stanley Bullock and telephonist Jean Pearce in the control room at the new ambulance headquarters, October 1968.

The WRAF Central Band marching past the Town Hall in September 1955 where the salute was taken by the Mayor.

Wolverhampton CID laboratory at Dunstall Road station. Detective Sergeant L.Whitehouse, left, with Police Cadet Guy Adams, check a piece of glass for fingerprints in December 1966.

The fire brigade of the early 1900s. The first brigade was formed in 1855.

Pictured in 1966, HM Inspector of Constabulary, Mr J.Manuel (third right) with Chief Superintendent P.D.Peterson (second right) and Mr N.Goodchild, Chief Constable of the new West Midland Police Force, look at the cycle patrol section during inspection.

Wolverhampton Ambulance Station, August 1969.

The Royal Hospital

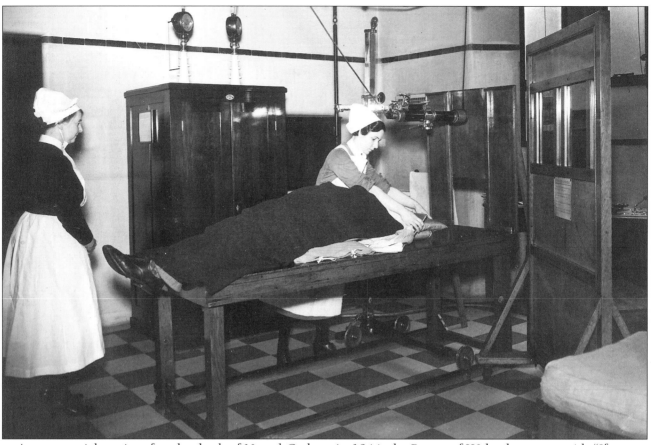

At a memorial service after the death of Norval Graham in 1944, the Rector of Wolverhampton said: "If you would see his memorial you will look at the Royal Hospital." This is the Radiographic Room in the early 1930s.

The waiting room, early 1930s.

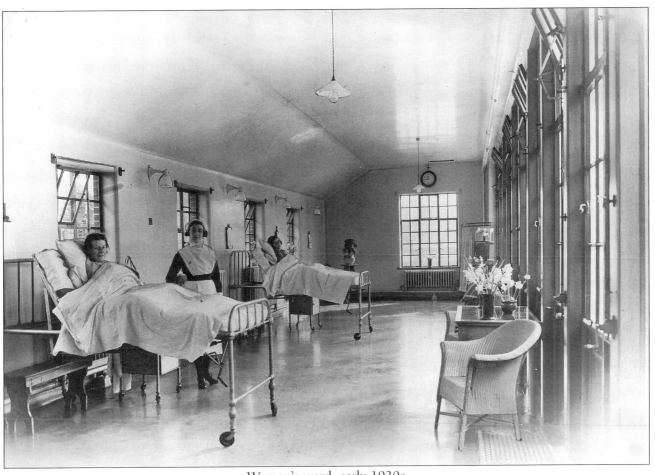

Women's ward, early 1930s.

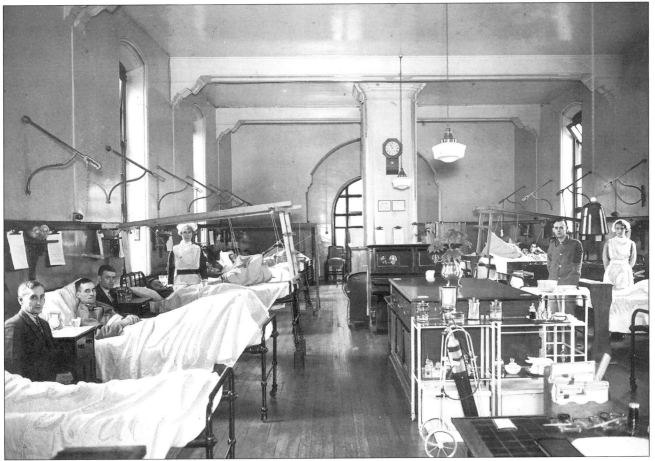

Men's ward, early 1930s.

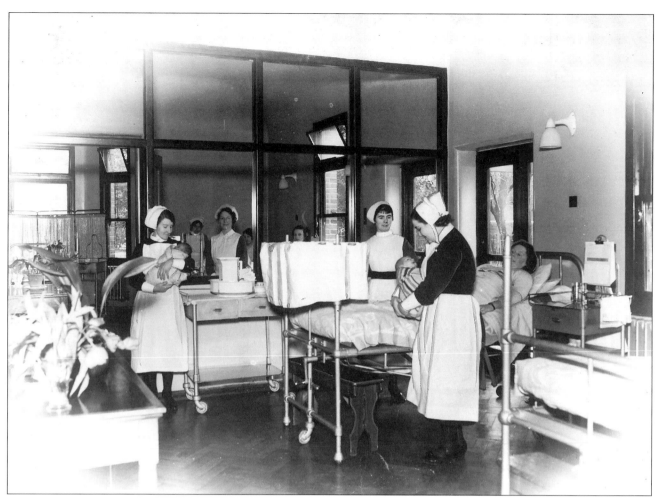

The Maternity
ward, early 1930s.

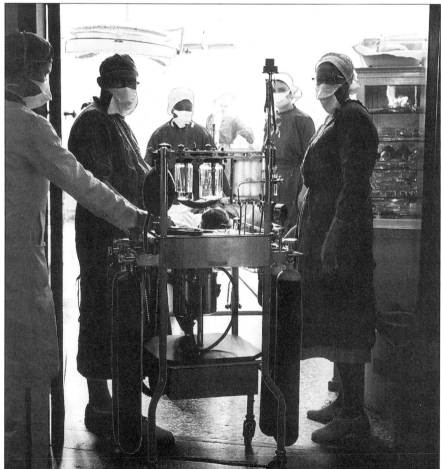

An anaesthetised
patient is wheeled
into the theatre in
September 1958.

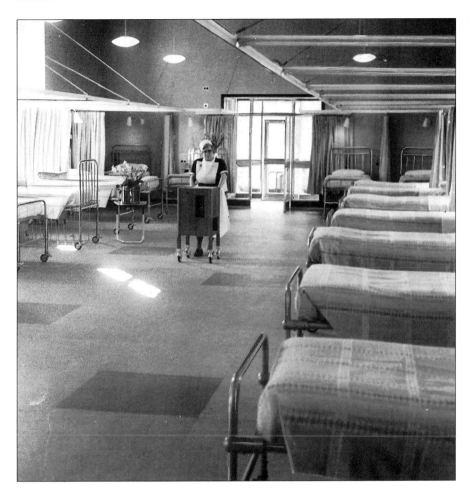

The Dartmouth Ward of the Royal Hospital after extensive alterations in February 1962.

District nurses' home around the early 1940s.

In May 1964 several hundred sightseers watched as an RAF helicopter from Tern Hill landed at the Royal Hospital to transfer a miner to Stoke Mandeville Hospital. News of the landing – the first ever made at the Royal – had spread like wildfire through the town.

The helicopter from RAF Tern Hill landing in the car-park at the rear of the hospital to transfer the injured miner.

The Royal Hospital, which was opened in 1849, pictured in March 1961.

Famous Folk

Percy Stallard, founder of the British League of Racing Cyclists and a pioneer of road racing in this country, is pictured congratulating his son Mick in January 1963 on being picked to ride for England – an honour he was accorded many times.

Hugh Porter in action in 1970, the same year he won the World Professional Cycling Championships held in Leicester.

Ace sprinter Peter Radford, a former Tettenhall College student, is seen sprinting home to win the 100 yards in 9.6 seconds in June 1961. He later went on to capture an Olympic medal.

International prima donna soprano Maggie Teyte, who was born in Wolverhampton, pictured around 1943.

The 'N Betweens pictured in December 1964. They later became better known as Slade.

Slade pictured in 1970.

A group of Wolverhampton Amateur Boxing Club members pictured in October 1962.

Members of the Wolverhampton
and District Old Time Boxers
Association, seen at Courtaulds'
Social Club in May 1962.

P.T.Stallard (left)
and R.Jones with
the machines they
rode at the
Copenhagen World
Amateur
Championships in
1937. Both riders
were from
Wolverhampton.

Mr James Beattie, founder of James Beattie Ltd, is pictured in the 1920s greeting Miss D.Hilton, while his sister, Miss C.Beattie, meets Miss V.Hilton at Wolverhampton Picture House. The Hiltons were famous Siamese twins.

Millionaire industrialist John Sangster at the wheel of an Ariel car with Wolverhampton-born Sir Charles Hayward in November 1969.

Miss Daisy St Clair Mander *en route* to Moscow to watch Wolves play Spartak in August 1955. Miss Mander's father was the late Sir Charles Mander, who was Wolves club president for over 20 years. On the extreme right in the picture is Miss Mander's nephew, also Sir Charles.

Sir Charles Wheeler, Wolverhampton-born sculptor and president of the Royal Academy, in October 1960 views the plaque on the house where he was born in Codsall. He is seen here left, with the chairman of Seisdon Rural District Council, Councillor G.Woodward. Sir Charles was the first sculptor to have been the Royal Academy president.

Groups and Organisations

Members of the Wolverhampton WVS pack gifts for distribution to local children in 1961.

Gathering of the RAOB Crusaders Lodge in 1926.

Audience in
February 1961 at
the Cliff Richard
Show at the
Gaumont.

Teenagers gathered round a telephone box at Brewood Square in October 1966.

The Young Elizabethan Girls Choir pictured in September 1954.

Mrs R.Staniforth, who was the accompanist, to the Boulton Paul Male Voice Choir, was the only woman at their 25th anniversary dinner in March 1968.

The Boulton Paul Aircraft Male Voice Choir presented their 25th anniversary concert at the Wulfrun Hall in October 1968. Conducting the choir was Mr J.Cleevely.

Royal Visitors

HRH the Duke of Gloucester at Low Hill, June 1939.

The Queen Mother visiting the kindergarten of the Royal School, 1969.

The Queen Mother leaving the Town Hall, 1969.

The Queen presents a guidon to the Staffordshire Yeomanry (Queen's Own Royal Regiment) during the military ceremony at the Molineux Grounds in May 1962.

The Queen inspects the troops on parade at Molineux, 1962.

The Queen being presented to Sir Norman Brook, Secretary of the Cabinet and a distinguished old boy of the Wolverhampton Grammar School, by the headmaster Mr E.R. Taylor during her visit to the school for the 450th anniversary celebrations in May 1962.

In 1943 the Duke of Gloucester visited the Royal Hospital, Wolverhampton. Front row (left to right): The Mayor of Wolverhampton (Councillor A.Byrne-Quinn), the Duke of Gloucester, Matron (Miss M.Millar).

The Duke of Gloucester, Earl of Shrewsbury and the Mayor of Wolverhampton at the Municipal Airport, June 1939.

The Prince of Wales, later Edward VIII then the Duke of Windsor, visits the Royal Hospital, Wolverhampton, 1923.

HRH The Duke of York at Molineux Grounds, Wolverhampton, 1922.

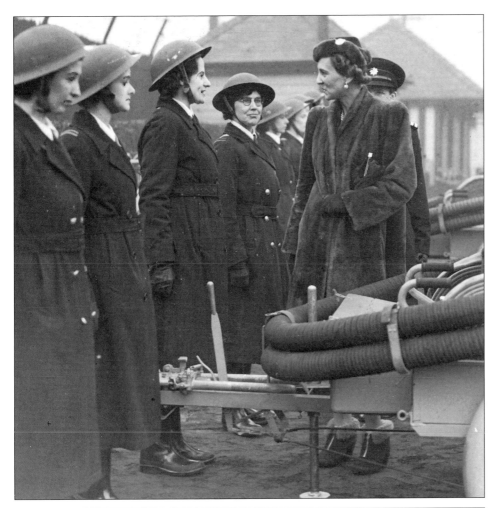

The Duchess of Kent inspecting some of the members of Wolverhampton Women's NFS detachment who staged an incident at Monmore Green greyhound racing stadium in December 1941.

The Duke of York (later King George VI), left, at a local function returning a salute to a schoolgirl at Molineux Gardens, July 1922.

Queen Elizabeth takes her first look at Wolverhampton on her arrival by train in April 1940. George VI is talking to the Earl of Dudley and behind is the Mayor of Wolverhampton, Councillor H.A.White.

Princess Royal at Wolverhampton YMCA in July 1960. David White is seen meeting the Princess. The occasion was the opening of the new YMCA premises.

Crowds gathered in Wolverhampton Square for the proclamation of King George V in May 1910.

The Princess Royal arriving at Dunstall Park racecourse in October 1949 on an 'unofficial' visit to watch her three-year-old colt, Orphean, run. She is seen being met by Lord Willoughby de Roke, chairman of Wolverhampton Racecourse and Dunstall Park Club Company Ltd.

Queen Mary photographed at Patshull with the Earl and Countess of Dartmouth, with Lady Barbara Legge (left) and Lady Josceline Legge standing behind.

Tettenhall Wood school children waving to Queen Mary as she passed through the village in July 1939 after visiting Mary Lady Mander, at The Mount, Compton.

The Princess Royal leaving Bilston Town Hall in March 1946 with Councillor C.Holt Green. On the right is Miss Mander, Divisional Girl Guide Commissioner.

Town at War

Women at the WVS Depot at Tettenhall sorting out shoes supplied by the Lord Mayor of London's Fund for the use of blitzed people in March 1945.

Some of the victims of the air raid on Willenhall being buried in November 1940. Large crowds assembled and Civil Defence workers paid their tributes.

Prince Bernhard watching Dutch troops in training at Wrottesley Park during a wartime summer.

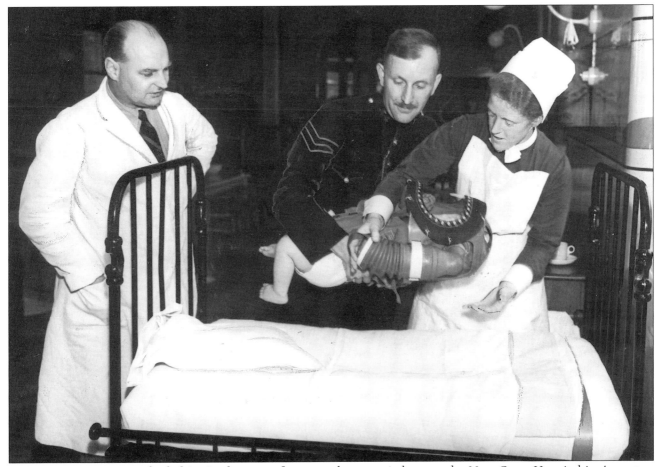

A protective covering for babies in the case of gas attacks was tried out at the New Cross Hospital in August 1939. The photograph shows Sergeant Stonier placing a child wearing one of the new coverings on a bed watched by Dr J.E.S.Lee, resident medical practitioner at the hospital, and a nurse.

Wolverhampton's fire-fighting float which was used on the canals during World War Two.

A fire caused by a bomb dropped during an air raid on Reynolds Restaurant, in Queen Square in March 1939 was soon put under control by the fire brigade.

Barmaid Elsie Dale at work turning out AA shell components in October 1941.

In May 1942, members of the Home Guard swam a race in full kit at the first annual swimming gala of the First Cadet Battalion South Staffordshire Regiment at Heath Town Baths. The winner was Lieutenant A.L.S.Harman, on the extreme left.

Women plate layers at work in December 1943.

VJ Celebrations, 16 August 1945 at Weston Park.

Evacuated school children from London arriving in Wolverhampton in July 1944.

Taken at Wolverhampton Riding School around 1913, this photograph shows the 4th Battery, Royal Field Artillery.

Crowds lined the streets to welcome back local servicemen returning home from the Boer War in 1902.

Members of Wolverhampton Home Guard unit held a tank-stopping exercise in May 1941. Here they are with the crew of the car used to represent the tank.

A familiar sight on the streets of Wolverhampton in May 1942 were women bus drivers.

A view from the old Waterloo Road Stand at Molineux, taken in May 1945 showing children taking part in the
Wolverhampton schoolchildren's victory thanksgiving service.

Dutch seamen on parade at a United Nations service held at the Molineux Grounds on 14 June 1942.

Earl Harrowby takes the salute at the march-past at Molineux. On the extreme left is Colonel N.C.Joseph (Zone Commander) and also in the group is Major Lord Dartmouth and the Mayor, Councillor A.Byrne-Quinn.

Spring Street Youth Club celebrate VE Day, 8 May 1945.

VE Day street party, Regent Road.

Getting Around

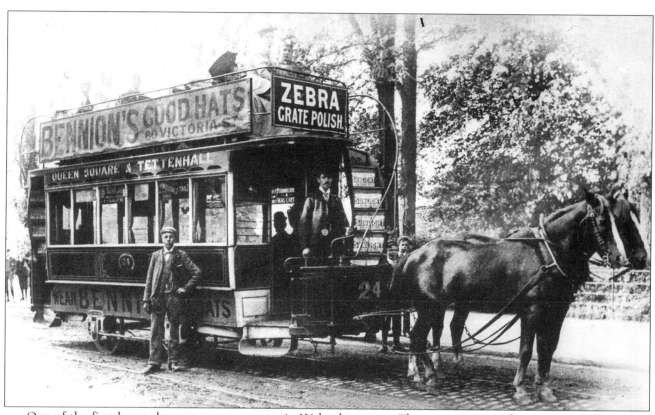

One of the first horse-drawn trams to appear in Wolverhampton. The trams ran to Bilston, Tettenhall and Willenhall from 1897 to 1900.

A larger than usual trolley bus which was made by Sunbeam Trolley Bus Co Ltd., in September 1954.

An early ambulance built by Fleming & Son of Cleveland Road, Wolverhampton.

Rush hour trolley buses in Wolverhampton's town centre in 1964.

Wolverhampton's first trolley bus, built in 1923, pictured at the top of Broad Street.

When this bus, *en route* for Penn Fields, carried it first passenger load in 1904, even the cabby's 'bus' stopped in astonishment.

Some of the last trolley buses seen in service in Wolverhampton in the early 1960s.

The rear-end double-decker bus which Wolverhampton Corporation tried out in August 1961.

Wolverhampton's Low Level Railway Station took on a bright and airy look in March 1962, well in time for the
Queen's visit on May 24.

The Low Level Station pictured in August 1969.

A crowded platform at Wolverhampton High Level Railway Station in April 1955 as holidaymakers waited for a Blackpool train.

Sunbeam motorcycle 347cc OHV, built around 1928 and the Sunbeam motorcycle 493cc OHV also built around 1928.

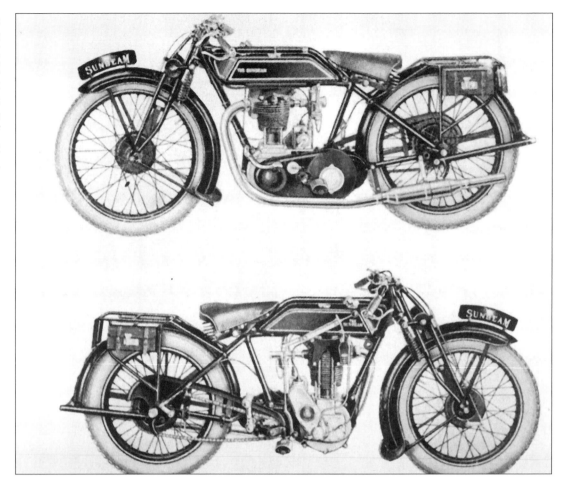

A Star motorcycle.

A 1922 Guy truck which was pensioned off in 1951 after delivering coal for nearly 30 years. The truck was built by Guy Motors which was based in Wolverhampton.

On 28 September 1955 this original Guy welded armoured car was put on display at the Imperial War Museum in London. It revolutionised armoured vehicle construction and is estimated to have saved £100,000 in wartime production costs. Guys were awarded £5,000 tax free by the Royal Commission of Awards after the war.

A Guy Invincible 24-ton eight-wheel tank pictured in August 1956.

A four-wheel bonneted type Guy Invincible MK II powered by a Gardner diesel engine at the Izmir International
Trade Fair in September 1959.

In most respects a truly local product. Manders Paints, Wolverhampton, half of whose fleet were Guys in July 1967, had recently placed in service this Big J.

A Ministry of Food vehicle which was used in World War Two and was made by Guy Motors.

In 1930 this Silver Bullet, made by Sunbeam Motor Car Co., Ltd, was driven by Mr Kaye Don at Daytona in an unsuccessful attempt to beat the world's land speed record.

Albrighton milkmen in the 1930s.

Mr Leonard Sneyd beside his lorry when he worked for the Bilston Gas Company in 1923.

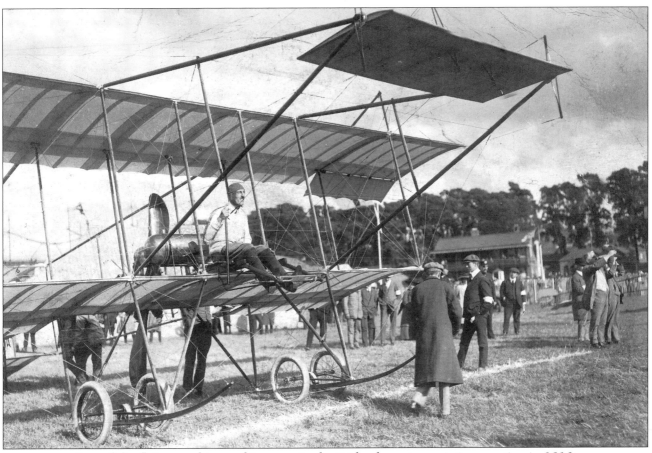

One of the flying machines taking part in the Wolverhampton aviation meeting in 1910.

Colonel J.H.Cooke, first chairman of the Midland Aero Club, Mrs Cooke and Miss Cooke, standing by a primitive aeroplane at Wolverhampton aviation meeting at Dunstall Park in June 1910.

Telling the News

Part of the composing room in the early 1930s. A battery of Linotype machines are seen on the left and right. The men in the foreground are setting headlines by hand.

In May 1954 the *Express & Star* held a photographic exhibition at Beatties store, Wolverhampton. This picture shows a section of the many visitors at the display.

Between 1918 and 1925 Georgian houses in Queen Street were bought to become the main office block for the *Express & Star*.

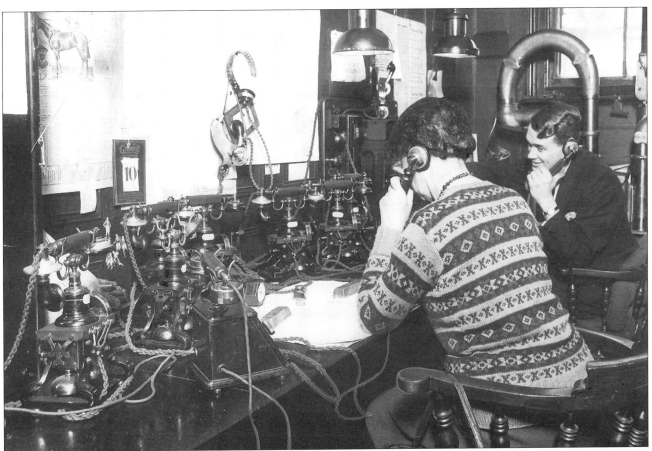

Copytakers in the late 1920s dealing with a mass of hand-held telephones. News items were often taken in shorthand and transcribed.

The stone – where type was assembled in the page formes in the early 1930s.

A corner of the four-man sub-editorial table in about 1928.

The *Express & Star* advertising section in 1959.

A cheer for the Prime Minister Mr Harold Macmillan at Tettenhall Green on his way to visit the *Express & Star*.

Malcolm Graham, standing in basket on left, about to take the *Express & Star's* first aerial photographs in the 1920s.

The *Express & Star* front office in the 1930s.

A fleet of vans being prepared to deliver the *Express & Star* in July 1959.

The front office in the late 1930s/early 1940s.

Reporters at work on Friday, 3 May 1967.

The Composing Room in the late 1930s/early 1940s.

New techniques
being applied to
conserve space in
the storage of
valuable records in
the newspaper's
new library in
1957.

Mr Joe Howells, who answered customers' queries for over 20 years, in April 1961.

The publishing department members prepare the newspaper for distribution to newsagents and the public in May 1963.

Making its first appearance in June 1969 was a replica of the horse-drawn waggons used around the turn of the century to deliver copies of the *Express & Star*.

The *Express & Star* library in the
early 1930s.

Special delivery…
this is one of the
Halfpenny Green
newsboys pictured
as he brought in
copies of the
Express & Star by
parachute in
August 1970.

Memorials

War Memorial in the churchyard of Tettenhall Parish Church, November 1966.

September 1969 saw a memorial plaque unveiled and dedicated at Lanesfield British Legion. The plaque was presented by Lanesfield British Legion women's section in memory of those who died while fighting for their country.

Pillar in St Peter's Church in the 1930s dedicated to an ancient Saxon Chief.

War Memorial in St Peter's Square, November 1966.

War Memorial in Wombourne churchyard, November 1966.

Lady Wulfruna Well. This stone was put in 1901 by local barrister and politician Alexander Staveley Hill, who was Lord of the Manor of Oxley. It marks the site of a spring associated with Lady Wulfruna, founder and benefactor of Wolverhampton, who is thought to have lived near Dunstall over 1,000 years ago.

Memorial in the gardens of St Peter's in honour of Douglas Morris Harris, hero of the *Floandi*. He was killed by enemy gunfire in the Adriatic Sea in May 1917.

FOR
EVERY
HOUR
THAT
COMES
THERE
IS A
HOPE

The clock at Tettenhall Rock pictured in 1969. It was donated by Mr and Mrs Edward Swindley of the Cedars, Tettenhall, to the Urban District of Tettenhall in June 1911 to commemorate the Coronation of His Majesty King George V. The Swindleys also donated the land lying between The Wergs and the cricket pitch to the people of Tettenhall.

The Wolves

Wolverhampton Wanderers' stand after a gale on 4 January 1925.

The scene of enthusiasm at Molineux after the close of the match against Port Vale which saw Wolves win the 1932 Second Division championship.

The FA Cup-winning Wolverhampton Wanderers squad of 1893. The team beat Everton in the Final which was held at Fallowfield in Manchester, the first time it had been played outside London.

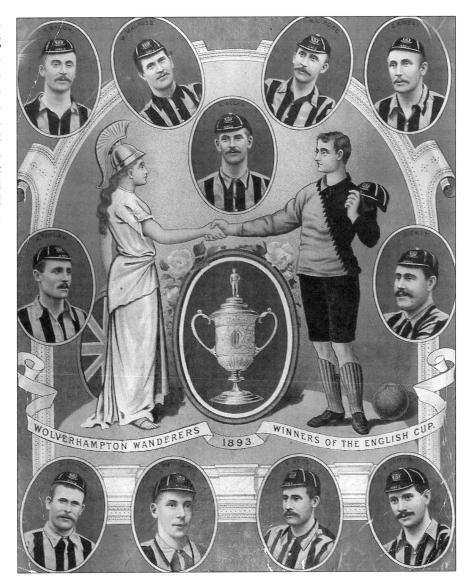

Wolverhampton Wanderers 1905-06.

Building of the new 146ft floodlighting towers at Molineux football ground beginning in July 1957. This picture taken from Waterloo Road shows the crane placing the girders into position. It was claimed that this new floodlighting system would give Wolves the best in the country outside Wembley.

Right: Wolverhampton Wanderers 1908.

Far Right: Stan Cullis gained 12 England caps before the war, played in 20 Victory and Wartime internationals and later managed Wolves to League and FA Cup successes.

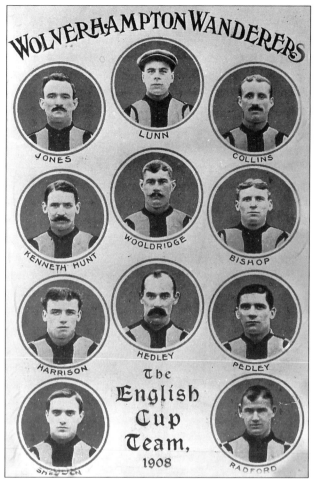

Wolverhampton Wanderers, 1893.

Wolverhampton Wanderers 1907.

Manager Stan Cullis shows off the 1953-54 League championship trophy to his winning team.

Wolverhampton Wanderers' 1923-24 Third Division North championship-winning team.

Crowds gathered outside the *Express & Star* office to discover the result of the FA Cup Final in 1908.

Wolves with the FA Cup in 1949. They beat Leicester City in the Final.

Billy Wright heads the winning Cup squad of 1949.

Cameramen scampered to get a final picture of England's great footballer Billy Wright on his last game for Wolves in August 1959. He had asked for no demonstrations. A wave to his friends – on the field and off – and he was gone. So ended the reign of the soccer King.

A triumphant Wolves team is carried by coach through the cheering thousands who greeted them after their FA Cup Final victory over Blackburn Rovers at Wembley in 1960.

The Duke of Gloucester being introduced to members of the Wolves team before the start of the FA Cup Final against Leicester in April 1949.

Wolves, League Championship winners in 1953-54.

Ron Flowers leads
Wolves into action
for the final time
during his
testimonial game
against an England XI
in October 1970.

Molineux seen
from the floodlight
pylons in January
1967.

Bill Slater introduces the Wolves to the Duke of Gloucester before the start of the FA Cup Final of 1960.

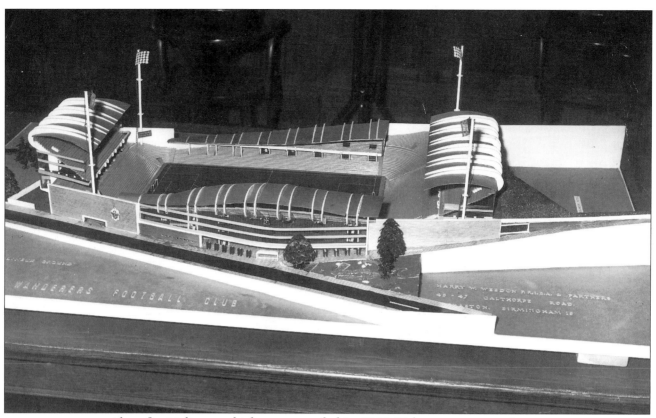

Plans for Molineux which were unveiled in 1960-61 but never came about.

Alterations at Molineux in May 1932.

Flying High

Flying only a few feet above the spectators' heads, the Vulcan bomber was one of the highlights of an air display held in June 1963 at Wolverhampton Airport. Later disaster was narrowly averted as the Blackburn Beverley of Transport Command, skimmed the boundary hedge.

Wolverhampton Flying Club display June 1948.

Wolverhampton Aero Club coat of arms.

Flying over the club house of Wolverhampton Aero Club were the Red Arrows at an air display at Pendeford airfield in June 1965.

A group of Wolverhampton Aero Club members pictured before taking part in the Royal Aero Club's annual Deauville rally in June 1963.

Pilots being briefed for the King's Cup air race at Wolverhampton Airport in June 1950.

Wolverhampton Airport seen from the air in April 1956.

Youthful Endeavour

Scouts from Wolverhampton and district setting out for the 1947 jamboree at Moissons, near Paris.

Hoisting the Colours Ceremony by the 10th Wolverhampton Sea Scouts at their headquarters at Newbridge under the command of Group Scoutmaster E.W.Williams and Assistant Scoutmaster R.J.Buckingham in July 1945.

To mark the end of Girl Guide Week, a parade was held at Willenhall in May 1939.

Some of the 70 Wolverhampton Boys Scouts who were appearing on the stage at the Gaumont Cinema in September 1938.

Left: The Eagle Parade of the 25th Wolverhampton (Our Lady) Scout Troop had just won the Archbishop's Flag in July 1947. The Scouts who gained this coveted award are from left to right: P.Roebuck, patrol leader, J.Spelman, A.S.A.Jones, M.Mason, J.Phillips; kneeling D.O'Brien, and M.Spelman.

Camping in September 1963 were the 1st Sedgley and 20th Wolverhampton cubs at Beaudesert Scout camp.

Four Girl Guides from the Coseley Company received gold and silver Duke of Edinburgh Awards at Darkhouse Baptist Church, Coseley in October 1969. Pictured from left, Miss L.Turley, the company's captain, Lynne Hughes, Eileen Paskin, the Mayor and Mayoress, Karen Shipley and Susan Jones.

To celebrate their Diamond Jubilee the Wolverhampton Division of the Girl Guides head a 'camp fire' singsong in the the Civic Hall in September 1970.

Exchanges with Tilburg

Wolverhampton children being handed their music sheets by Dr Young before leaving Wolverhampton High Level station to sing at Tilburg in May 1946.

Members of the Tilburg party, including Mayor, Alderman W.Lawley, returning to Wolverhampton after their visit to Tilburg.

Crowds of Wolverhampton people gathered to greet the Dutch party from Tilburg in August 1946. A number of events had been arranged in order that Wolverhampton people were able to reciprocate the hospitality they had enjoyed while visiting Holland earlier in the year.

Among events organised during the exchange of 1948 was a English-Dutch swimming gala at the Central Baths, Wolverhampton. This photograph shows Alan Treen being presented with a laurel wreath for his success. He is being congratulated by, left to right, Betty Westworth, Pam Rosser, Jill Cook, Thelma Butler, Peggy Brookes (coach, standing at rear), Alan Treen, Freda Holt and Philip Cook.

Wolverhampton and Tilburg tennis players pictured before their match at Newbridge in 1946.

Baron van Voorst tot
Voorst, the Burgomeister
of Tilburg, visited the
Central Baths of
Wolverhampton in
August 1948 to see a
swimming gala. He is
seen in the picture with
four of Wolverhampton's
county swimmers. They
are, from left to right,
Peggy Laurie, Hazel Pace,
Betty Westworth, and Jill
Cook.

On returning home after
their visit in 1946 the
Burgomeister of Tilburg,
Dr E.H.Baron van Voorst
tot Voorst and his wife
were presented with the
Mayor of Wolverhampton's
bike to dispose of as they
wished. The Mayor's son,
Private John Lawley, is
pictured presenting it.

A display of billiards at Fisher Bearings Sports and Social Club where an informal evening was held for the Tilburg visitors in 1948. Photograph shows Mr George Dallow trying his hand.

A civic reception was held at the Civic Hall for the visitors from Tilburg in 1946.

Wolverhampton and Tilburg children broadcasting from the Midlands studios of the BBC in Birmingham in 1946. At the microphone is Miss Margaret Bacon, on the right Mr Percy Edgar, Midland Regional Director, and the Mayor and Mayoress of Wolverhampton.

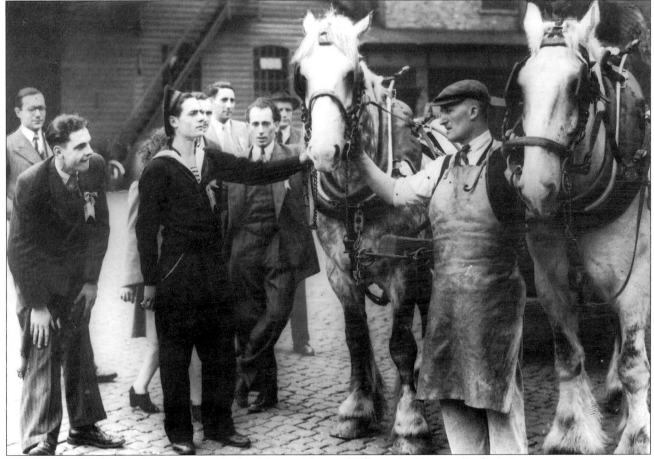

A pair of greys were admired from visitors of Tilburg in 1946 at Butler's Brewery.

Subscribers

Mr A C Adams
Mr R L Allden
R V & P M Aris
A Arrowsmith
H Atkinson
V Atkinson
C Baggott
Sidney T Baker MBE
Judy Banks
D Barlow
S A Barnett
Mrs B Bate
T H Beach
Martin Beddall B Eng
Mr B Bellingham
David Bennett
Mr & Mrs K Berks
Betty Berry
James A Billson
Mr & Mrs Bird
John Blakemore
Pat Blakemore
Barry Bond
Frances E Bookham
Dr Paul Boyle
G R Brazier
Elizabeth Bridgewood
M D Bright
Mrs A M Brooks
Mrs J A Brooks-Davies
Mr & Mrs E L Broomhall
Beryl M Buck
Lt Cdr M J Buckley RN
Mrs D M Bucknall
Mrs D B Bunce
M Campbell
O E Canning
A J Carter
Ronald Edward Carter
Ronald Edward Carter
M J Cartwright
J Challenger
J Challenger
Mrs B Cheese
Mr Peter Chinn

Mrs E E Churchman
John Alfred Clarke
G Clinton
Brian F Cookson
Edward Cooper
Jean Cooper
Rachel Cooper
J Corns
H Cotterill
John H Cox
O M Cox
Thomas Cox
K Cullen
Les Dando
Dorothy Grace Darbey
M & E Darlington
O & S Darlington
A Davis
Mr A J Dawson
R Dawtry
Cyril Day
C S Dean
K J Dean
A Dixon
H J W Dodd
Mr & Mrs B L Drew (Kitchener, Canada)
David R Dungar
C Dutton
G R Edgley
John Edwards
Eric Evans
G Farmer
Mrs Farr
R Fincher
E V Ford
Mrs Iris Forde
Michael Forde
John M Foster
A J Giddings
Glennis Giles
Terence Giles
Mr D Gladwin
Blanche Goode
Mr Stephen Goodey
B Goodman
Julia Govan
D & C Graham
John Grainger

L W Green
Arthur Griffiths
Cliff Griffiths
Mrs Edwina Griffiths
G Griffiths
Merle Guest
K M Hall
L Hallett
L Hallett
J P Hampton
Geoff Hancock
Fred Handy
Susan Hart
O F Hartland
Ian Harvey
Margaret Hewitt
Margaret Hewitt
Mr F S Hickie
William John Hickman
Clive Hilton
Robert Hodgkiss
G L Hollingworth
J Holloway
D M Horovitz
J Hough
Mrs I E Huntley
A W Huntley
I Huselbee
Mrs Patricia Hustin
J W Hutchings
Mr & Mrs T J Image
B A Jackson
T C Jackson
G Jenkins
William F Jevons
Arthur G Jones
Gordon A Jones
Lee Jones
Paul Jones
Margaret Joyce
D Keeling
May Elizabeth Kemp
Mrs Marie Kimberley
R J Lane
Mark Leadbetter
F J Leese
Wilfred Lewis
Pat Lilley

Trevor Lloyd
Mrs P A Lockett
D Lockley
D J Lockley
R B Lycett
Mr R B McCutcheon
R P McKenna
T L McLachlan
John McNish
Christine McQuillan
G R Manning
Wendy Mansell
J L Mantle
Geoffrey Marchant
Michael F Marren
D R Marshall
David J Matthews
W G Meredith
Ray Millington
John N Mills
Annita Mobbs
Alan Moore
A R Moore
R J Mountford
T H Morris
J H Nason
Paul O'Donoghue
Jean O'Toole
B W Page
Raymond Page
Mr George Parker
Alan Parkes
W Parkes
R Parnwell
Sharda Patel
Frank Pepworth
Frank Percival
Mr C K Perks
Mr Michael Maurice Perks
J Perry
Colin Pinches
Violet Pinfield
Rose Potts
Margaret Powell
Prescott
Agnes Price
Barry E Price
Mrs L Price

Irene & Geoff Pritchard
C A Reade
Ian Redmond
Mr Colin R Richards
Mr R A Richards
Mr D W Rickhuss
Mr P R Rivett
Mrs K Roberts
Mrs K Roberts
Mr W A J Roberts
William J Roberts
Mr Charlie Robinson
John Edwin Rock
Mrs B Rollason
Peter Round
Dr M H A Russell
E Rutter
Adam James Sambrook
Mr B Sandbrook
G & J Sedgwick
Cllr D M Seiboth
Mr I J D Sharp
J A Sharples
Mrs D Smith
Mrs H O Smith
Sheila Smith
William Smith
A Southall
J E Spratt
Anthony Stafford
Michael Stanley
C Stokes
John H Stubbs
Clive Styles
R Summers
S Sumner
Laurence Swift
Pat Tabner
Pat Tabner
R G Taylor
C E Taylor-Hutchinson
Joyce Thomas
Beryl Till
R F Till
Pamela Tonks
J A D Trask
Arnold Walker
Mr G A Walker

Mr R Ward
Tom Watts
John Henry Wesley
B Whitehall
B Wilcox
G J Wilde
J A Wilde
Pat Wilde
Pat Wilde
Mr Reg Wildig
Betty Williams
Mrs F M Williams
James Williams
Jean Williams
M Williams
Ned Williams
Mr & Mrs Peter Williams
Mr Roger Williams
V Williams
J Withers
R W M Wollaston
Wolverhampton Archives & Local Studies
Mr Brian Wood
Wood End P School
Richard G Woodruff
David L Woolf
Gregory S Worwood
Doylan L Worwood
Janet Wright
Mr & Mrs J T Wright
Kenneth R Wright
J Van-Leerzem